Prayers
For All Occasions

PRAYERS FOR ALL OCCASIONS

This companion to *Prayers New and Old* is intended to provide prayers not only for private devotions but also for particular needs and events in the life of the Church and of the nation. The Index gives a convenient guide to prayers for special occasions. It is hoped, furthermore, that this collection will also help to meet the needs of those who wish to plan their private devotions more systematically.

There is widespread uneasiness and dissatisfaction among Christian people concerning their prayers. The reasons for this are various, but there is one in particular which is undoubtedly common: prayers are not properly organized, nor made a solemn and deliberate act of worship, carefully thought out and prepared in advance.

There are, of course, times in everyone's life when prayer cannot wait to be organized; no plan of prayer will serve then. But normally people do need a plan, a method of devotion, and it is intended that this book may help to meet this need.

The *Amen* is a liturgical ending and has no place in private prayer. We have also omitted the usual Christian ending—*through Jesus Christ our Lord*—from most of the private prayers, since it is sufficient if this is said at the close of the act of devotion.

CONTENTS

PLAN FOR MORNING DEVOTIONS

(The reading of a passage from the Bible, or the daily meditation in *Forward—day by day* should always form part of morning or evening devotions.)

1. Hold the mind for a few seconds in silent recollection of the presence of God, saying slowly: *O God, who art present in every place, help me to realize thy presence here and now.*
2. An act of praise and adoration. See pages 5-6.
3. Prayer for spiritual strength and guidance for the day, followed by dedication to the doing of God's will, and an affirmation of sincere intention. See pages 6-8.
4. Brief intercession for family and friends, and for any seriously sick or bereaved.
5. The Lord's Prayer.
6. Great value will be found in the slow repetition of such passages of Scripture as: *In quietness and in confidence shall be your strength. Thou wilt keep him in perfect peace whose mind is stayed on thee.*

   I am not alone, for the Father is with me.

PLAN FOR EVENING DEVOTIONS

1. The same as the morning.
2. An act of thanksgiving. See page 11.
3. Confession of sin and prayer for forgive-

ness. This should be in one's own words, with specific mention of known sins. But see also page 18.

4. Intercession. More time should be given to this than in the morning, and a scheme of intercessions might be arranged for a week. For subjects other than those of a private character see Contents, page 3. The Mission of the Church should have a place in every churchman's prayers.

5. The Lord's Prayer and the Gloria Patri.

ACTS OF PRAISE AND ADORATION

Glory be to God on high, and on earth peace, good will towards men. We praise thee, we bless thee, we worship thee, we glorify thee, we give thanks to thee for thy great glory . . . .

Blessed art thou, O Lord God of our fathers: praised and exalted above all for ever.

Holy, Holy, Holy, Lord God of hosts, Heaven and earth are full of thy glory: Glory be to thee, O Lord most high.

We praise thee, O God; we acknowledge thee to be the Lord. . . . And we worship thy Name ever, world without end.

Praise the Lord, O my soul; and all that is within me, praise his only Name.

5

Blessed be thou, O God, who hast given us the light of the knowledge of thy glory in the face of Jesus Christ.

Glory be to the Father, and to the Son, and to the Holy Ghost; as it was in the beginning, is now, and ever shall be, world without end.

AFFIRMATIONS OF FAITH AND SINCERE INTENTION

The Apostles' Creed

I believe in God the Father Almighty, Maker of heaven and earth:

And in Jesus Christ his only Son our Lord: Who was conceived by the Holy Ghost, Born of the Virgin Mary: Suffered under Pontius Pilate, was crucified, dead, and buried: He descended into hell; The third day he rose again from the dead: He ascended into heaven, And sitteth on the right hand of God the Father Almighty: From thence he shall come to judge the quick and the dead.

I believe in the Holy Ghost: The holy Catholic Church; The Communion of Saints: The Forgiveness of sins: The Resurrection of the body: And the Life everlasting. Amen.

Psalm 23

The Lord is my shepherd; I shall not want.

He maketh me to lie down in green pastures: he leadeth me beside the still waters.

He restoreth my soul: he leadeth me in the paths of righteousness for his name's sake.

Yeah, though I walk through the valley of the shadow of death, I will fear no evil: for thou art with me; thy rod and thy staff they comfort me.

Thou preparest a table before me in the presence of mine enemies: thou anointest my head with oil; my cup runneth over.

Surely goodness and mercy shall follow me all the days of my life: and I will dwell in the house of the Lord for ever.

Affirmations

Heavenly Father, thou hast made me thine, and I rejoice in the knowledge of thy love through Jesus Christ our Lord. I would live this day in love of thee and in obedience to thy holy will. Give me thy enabling grace.

Lord Jesus, I am pledged to be thy faithful soldier and servant to my life's end. In thy abiding presence is my strength; with thee as my constant companion I am fortified to meet the trials and temptations of the day.

As I abide in Christ I am supplied with all the spiritual resources for my needs.

As I abide in Christ I am free from fear and have quietness and confidence within.

As I abide in Christ I am at one with God and know the peace of God which passes understanding.

I can do all things through Christ who strengthens me.

I believe on the Son of God; therefore I am in him.

Having redemption through his blood and life by his Spirit.

He is in me and all fullness is in him.

To him I belong by creation, purchase, conquest, and self-surrender: to me he belongs for all my hourly need.

There is no difficulty inward or outward which he is not ready to meet in me today.

I believe I have received not the spirit of fearfulness, but of power and of love and of a sound mind.

The Lord is my keeper.

St. Patrick's Breastplate

I bind unto myself today
    The strong Name of the Trinity,
By invocation of the same,
    The Three in One, and One in Three.

I bind unto myself today
    The power of God to hold and lead,
His eye to watch, his might to stay,
    His ear to harken to my need;
The wisdom of my God to teach,
    His hand to guide, his shield to ward;
The word of God to give me speech,
    His heavenly host to be my guard.

DAILY PRAYERS

A Morning Prayer

I thank thee, O God, for keeping me through the night, and for the promise of this new day. I would begin it with thee, and pray that it may be to me a day of growth in the spirit and of service for thee and thy kingdom in the world. Help me to meet with quiet confidence whatever trials the day holds for me; strengthen me against temptation; and keep me always loyal to our Lord and Saviour Jesus Christ.

A Morning Commitment

I commit myself to God for today. By the help of his grace, I will endeavour to keep his commandments, and to follow faithfully in the way of Jesus Christ our Lord.

Noon

Blessed Saviour, who at this hour didst hang upon the cross stretching forth thy loving arms, grant that all mankind may look unto thee and be saved.

Almighty Saviour, who at mid-day didst call thy servant Saint Paul to be an apostle to the Gentiles; we beseech thee to illumine the world with the radiance of thy glory, that all nations may come and worship thee, who art with the Father and the Holy Ghost, one God, world without end.

Give peace for all time, O Lord, and fill my heart and the hearts of all men everywhere with the spirit of our Lord Jesus Christ.

Night

Our Father, the day is over and I turn to thee before I take my rest. Thou hast been with me all the day long, and for all thy mercies—perceived and unperceived—I give thanks. All that has been amiss in me, in thought, word and deed, I repent of, and do thou graciously forgive, as I also forgive all who have offended me. Grant me now the blessings of a quiet mind and a trustful spirit: the freedom from fear of a child in its father's house. So let me rest in thee, at peace with thee and with all men; through Jesus Christ our Lord.

I will lay me down in peace and take my rest; for thou, Lord, only, makest us to dwell in safety.

Thou, O Christ, art in the midst of us and we are called by thy Name; leave us not, O Lord our God.

Save us, O Lord, while waking, guard us while sleeping; that awake we may watch with Christ, and asleep we may rest in peace.

ACTS OF THANKSGIVING

We praise thee, O God, with gladness and humility for all the joys of life, for health and strength, for the love of friends, for work to do, and play to re-create us. We thank thee for the adventure of life. Above all, we thank thee for thy unspeakable gift of Jesus Christ our Lord, for the blessings that have come to us through his body the Church; and help us to show our thankfulness, not only with our lips, but in our lives, always endeavouring to do that which shall please thee; through Jesus Christ our Lord.

O God, the giver of all good gifts, we thank thee for all the blessings which we have. Give us always contented minds, cheerful hearts, and ready wills, so that we may spend and be spent in the service of others, after the example of him who gave his life a ransom for many, our Lord and Master, Jesus Christ.

We give thanks to thee, O Father,
for thy holy name which thou hast made to dwell in our hearts,
    and for the knowledge, and faith, and immortality, which thou hast given unto us through Jesus thy Son:
        To thee be glory forever.

Thou, Lord Almighty, hast created all things for thy name's sake,

and hast given food and drink to men for their enjoyment, that they might give thanks unto thee; and on us thou hast bestowed spiritual food and drink,

and eternal life through thy Son:

To thee be glory forever.

Remember, O Lord, thy Church,

to deliver it from all evil and to perfect it in thy love.

Sanctify it and gather it together into thy Kingdom which thou hast prepared for it.

For thine is the power and the glory for ever and ever.

Bless the Lord, O my soul: and all that is within me, bless his holy name.

Bless the Lord, O my soul, and forget not all his benefits:

Who forgiveth all thine iniquities; who healeth all thy diseases;

Who redeemeth thy life from destruction; who crowneth thee with loving-kindness and tender mercies. *Psalm 103:1-4*

While I live will I praise the Lord: I will sing praises unto my God while I have any being. *Psalm 146:2*

Giver of all good things, we thank thee: for health and vigour; for the air that gives the breath of life, the sun that warms us, and the good food that makes us strong; for happy homes and for the friends we love; for all that makes it good to live. Make us thankful, and eager to repay, by cheerfulness and kindliness, and by a readiness to help others. Freely we have received; let us freely give, in the name of him who gave his life for us, Jesus Christ our Lord.

Almighty God, Father of all mercies, we thine unworthy servants, do give thee most humble and hearty thanks for all thy goodness and loving-kindness to us, and to all men; We bless thee for our creation, preservation, and all the blessings of this life; but above all, for thine inestimable love in the redemption of the world by our Lord Jesus Christ; for the means of grace, and for the hope of glory. And, we beseech thee, give us that due sense of all thy mercies, that our hearts may be unfeignedly thankful; and that we show forth thy praise, not only with our lips, but in our lives, by giving up our selves to thy service, and by walking before thee in holiness and righteousness all our days; through Jesus Christ our Lord, to whom with thee and the Holy Ghost, be all honour and glory, world without end.

FAMILY PRAYERS

For the Family

Heavenly Father, we thank thee for thy mercies which are new every morning: for health and strength, for this day with its fresh opportunities for work and service. Bless each one of us, and hold us together in thy love and in love of thee. We pray for thy help and guidance as we face the duties to be done, the decisions to be made, the temptations that may beset us, the disappointments that may await us. Guide us, strengthen us, keep us; and grant that in all things we may act worthily of our Christian calling; through Jesus Christ our Lord.

Heavenly Father, in whom we live and move and have our being, we humbly pray thee so to guide and govern us by thy Holy Spirit, that in all the cares and occupations of our daily life we may never forget thee, but remember that we are ever walking in thy sight; through Jesus Christ our Lord.

For Children

O Lord Jesus Christ, who didst take children into thy arms and bless them, we pray thee to keep our children ever enfolded by thy love. Help them to grow into love of thee; save them from evil; strengthen them against the impulses of self-will; inspire in them a high sense of truth and of the duty of human service; and give them grace to follow day by day in the steps of thy most holy life.

A Boy's or Girl's Prayer

Heavenly Father, I thank thee for my father and mother and for our home. Bless us all, and help us to love thee, and in love to serve one another as Jesus taught us to do. Give me strength to do what is right today, and to do unto others as I would have them do unto me.

Prayers for a Little Child

Dear Father in Heaven, I thank you for Jesus, who came to bring us your love, and to teach us to love one another. Help me to love everybody and to do what he would like me to do.

Dear God, I thank you for all good things: for my home, for food and clothing, for my friends, for the flowers and trees and birds— and everything; and when I grow up help me to share all my good things with others.

For a Birthday

We thank thee, Heavenly Father, for all thy mercies during the years that are past, and pray for thy continued blessing through the days to come. As thou hast been mindful of us, so make us always mindful of thee. Our times are in thy hand, and thou art our hope and strength. Do thou, we beseech thee, abide with us, guide and keep us until at last we come to thine everlasting kingdom; through Jesus Christ our Lord.

GRACE BEFORE MEAL

Bless, O Lord, this food to our use and us to thy service, and keep us ever mindful of the needs of others; for Christ's sake.

For these and all his mercies God's holy Name be praised.

Blessed be the Lord daily for all his mercies; through Jesus Christ our Lord.

We thank thee, Lord, for our daily bread both for body and soul; and do thou keep us ever mindful of thy good providence; through Jesus Christ our Lord.

We give thanks to thee, Almighty God, for these thy earthly gifts. As our bodies are strengthened and refreshed, so may we be made strong in our souls to glorify thee in our lives; through Jesus Christ our Lord.

Bless and praise the Lord for his goodness.
The Lord be blessed and praised.

Thanks be to God to whom our thanks are due.
Thanks be to God for ever and ever.

PERSONAL PRAYERS

For Forgiveness

O Almighty Father, Lord of heaven and earth, we confess that we have sinned against thee in thought, word, and deed. Have mercy upon us, O God, after thy great goodness; according to the multitude of thy mercies, do away our offences and cleanse us from our sins; for Jesus Christ's sake.

Almighty God, I have sinned against thee, and in penitence pray for thy forgiveness. In thy mercy hear me, and give me strength to overcome my weakness and to live day by day according to thy holy will; through Jesus Christ our Lord.

Lord, I have sinned against my neighbor, and therefore also against thee. Forgive me, and grant me the humility and the courage to go and admit my fault and seek reconciliation, as our Master taught us to do. I ask this in his Name.

For Purity of Heart

Almighty God, unto whom all hearts are open, all desires known, and from whom no secrets are hid; Cleanse the thoughts of our hearts by the inspiration of thy Holy Spirit, that we may perfectly love thee, and worthily magnify thy holy Name; through Christ our Lord.

On Going to Work

Lord, be with me as I go to my work today. Help me to be faithful in the discharge of my duties, and honorable in all my dealings. Give me self-control in speech and temper; and let me be a good example to others of Christian humility and thoughtfulness, that so I may glorify thee.

For Those Whose Work is in the Home

Lord Jesus, born of Mary, help me to do all I have to do today as unto thee. Let my tasks be eased by the knowledge of thy presence, and of thy loving care for thine own. Give me a desire to do all things for love of thee; strength to meet without complaint the trials of the day; and a thankful heart for all God's mercies.

For a Child Going to School

Dear God, come with me to school and be with me in my lessons and in my play. Help me to be friendly and thoughtful for others, obedient to my teachers, careful in my studies, and like Jesus in my words and deeds.

For Youth in School and College

Lord Jesus, who in thy young manhood didst hear and obey the call to give thy life in sacrifice for the salvation of mankind and for the kingdom of God, help me in this time of my youth to discover how best I can serve God in my life. In my days of preparation at school, keep ever before my eyes the prize that is better than any earthly prize. Save me from material aims and ambitions, and direct me in all my studies that they may serve above all things to make me better prepared to do the work which thou wilt give me to do. Keep me day by day loyal to thee; strengthen me to resist the temptations of the body and the mind; and help me to influence others towards love of thee and thy holy Church.

For Those Advanced in Years

Heavenly Father, whose gift is length of days; Help us to make noble use of mind and body in our advancing years. As thou hast pardoned our transgressions, sift the in-gatherings of our memory that evil may grow dim and good may shine forth. We bless thee for thy gifts, and especially for thy presence and the love of friends in heaven and earth. Grant us new ties of friendship, new opportunities of service, joy in the growth and happiness of children, sympathy with those who bear the world's burdens, clear thought and quiet faith. Teach us to bear infirmities with cheerful patience. Keep us from narrow pride in outgrown ways, blind eyes that will not see the good of change, impatient judgments of the methods and experiments of others. Let thy peace rule our spirits through all the trial of our waning powers. Take from us all fear of death, and all despair or undue love of life, that with glad hearts at rest in thee we may await they will concerning us; through Jesus Christ our Lord.

For Grace in Speech

Help me, O Lord, to keep guard over my lips. Save me from words that hurt: from gossip and slander and lies. Let me speak only to encourage and cheer and to keep people on their feet, so that all my words may minister grace, to thy honor and glory.

In Time of Temptation

Lord and Master, Jesus Christ, who thyself wast tempted as we are, yet without sin, give me grace to meet this temptation which now assails me and which I would overcome. Enable me to check all evil thoughts and passions, all enticements to self-indulgence or dishonest gain, and to find, like thee, my highest satisfactions in the doing of my Heavenly Father's will.

For a Time of Decision

Heavenly Father, who hast promised the gift of thy Holy Spirit to those who ask it; I come to thee for light and direction now as I face the necessity of decision between the ways that lie before me. May thy Holy Spirit guide me in my uncertainty: saving me from self-will, and the placing of desire before the burden of responsibility. Let it be thy will, not mine, that I seek, and show me how I can both serve thee and fulfill my duty towards those dependent upon me. Give me wisdom in this hour, O Lord; and when I see thy way give me grace to follow in it.

For Guidance of the Holy Spirit

O God, forasmuch as without thee we are not able to please thee; mercifully grant that thy Holy Spirit may in all things direct and rule our hearts; through Jesus Christ our Lord.

For Loyalty in Discipleship

O Jesus Christ, the Lord of all good life, who hast called us to help build the city of God; do thou enrich and purify our lives and deepen in us our discipleship. Help us daily to know more of thee, and through us by the power of thy Spirit, show forth thyself to other men. Make us humble, brave and loving; make us ready for adventure. We do not ask that thou wilt keep us safe, but that thou wilt keep us loyal; who for us didst face death unafraid, and dost live and reign for ever and ever.

Teach us, good Lord, to serve thee as thou deservest; to give and not to count the cost; to fight and not to heed the wounds; to toil and not to seek for rest; to labor and not to ask for any reward, save that of knowing that we do thy will; through Jesus Christ our Lord.

For Love Toward God

O God, who hast prepared for those who love thee such good things as pass man's understanding; pour into our hearts such love toward thee, that we, loving thee above all things, may obtain thy promises, which exceed all that we can desire; through Jesus Christ our Lord.

O Thou who art the Light of the minds that know thee, the Life of the souls that love thee, and the Strength of the wills that serve thee; help us so to know thee that we may truly love thee, so to love thee that we may fully serve thee, whom to serve is perfect freedom; through Jesus Christ our Lord.

For Freedom From Anxiety

O most loving Father, who willest us to give thanks for all things, to dread nothing but the loss of thee, and to cast all our care on thee, who carest for us; preserve us from faithless fears and worldly anxieties, and grant that no clouds of this mortal life may hide from us the light of that love which is immortal, and which thou hast manifested unto us in thy Son, Jesus Christ our Lord.

For Peace of Mind

Lord, thou knowest my cares and my fears. Help me to turn them all over to thee, who hast promised to give rest to our souls. Grant to me now a restful spirit and a peaceful mind, and in quietness and confidence and faith to find new strength.

In Adversity

Almighty God, who hast promised that when we are passing through the waters thou wilt be with us, and that they shall not overflow us, do thou be my help and Saviour now in this time of trouble. I need thy grace and thy strong hand. Uphold me and do not let me fall into despair or bitterness or the mire of self-pity. Renew in me hope and faith; give me the assurance of thy presence, and courage to face bravely the trials of the days to come; through Jesus Christ our Lord.

In Sickness

O God my Father, hold me in thy keeping. Thou hast made my body and hast meant it to be whole. Be with me when I am bewildered by sickness and by pain. Let me trust the power of thy healing; and above all and through all let me trust thy love that does not fail. Give me back, I pray thee, health and vigor, that I may set my hands again with gladness to the unhindered tasks of life; but if this may not be, then teach me still to serve as best I can with bent or broken tools. May any suffering I must undergo teach me sympathy with all who suffer; and may every gift of life renewed send me forth with a thankful heart to greater consecration; through Jesus Christ my Lord.

In Bereavement

Almighty God, who hast taught us that they who mourn shall be comforted; grant that in all our grief we may turn to thee; and, because our need is beyond the help of men, grant us the peace of thy consolation and the joy of thy love; through Jesus Christ our Lord.

Heavenly Father, to whom all our sorrows are known, grant to me the comfort of thy grace in my loss and loneliness. I thank thee for the love that has been mine and that even now is mine, since we are still one in thee. Give me day by day strength to bear my burden, and help me to live in the light of the world to come until my life's end.

St. Francis' Prayer

O Lord, our Christ, may we have thy mind and thy spirit; make us instruments of thy peace; where there is hatred, let us sow love; where there is injury, pardon; where there is discord, union; where there is doubt, faith; where there is despair, hope; where there is darkness, light; and where there is sadness, joy.

O divine Master, grant that we may not so much seek to be consoled as to console; to be understood, as to understand; to be loved, as to love; for it is in giving that we receive; it is in pardoning that we are pardoned; and it is in dying that we are born to eternal life.

INTERCESSIONS

Plan for Intercessions for a Week

Sunday: For your Church: the clergy, lay officers, teachers and children in Church School, choir, women's organizations, secretaries, and sextons.

Monday: For your home, family, and relations, and for friends.

Tuesday: For the advancement of the Kingdom of God, all Christian leaders; the World Council and the National Council of Churches.

Wednesday: For your city or community. For the police, postmen, firemen and all other civic employees.

Thursday: For the Country: the President, national and state legislators; the men and women in the Armed Forces; leaders in industry and labor, and for cooperation and goodwill between them; and all who toil with hand or head.

Friday: For nations and peoples; the United Nations; for the end of rivalry and strife, and the achievement of lasting peace.

Saturday: For the sick and all the poor and suffering throughout the world; the handicapped, the seemingy incurable, the blind and deaf and dumb, widows and orphans; doctors, nurses, orderlies, chaplains, and

27

all who work in hospitals; the aged; displaced persons throughout the world; and those in prisons.

For Absent Ones and Travellers

O God, who art present in every place, we pray thee to enfold with thy loving care our dear ones who are away from us, and all who travel by land, sea or air. Let thy fatherly hand ever be over them; prosper them in their way; grant to them daily strength for their daily needs; and inspire in them an unwavering faith in thee, that they may live always to thy honour and glory.

For Those Shut-in and Isolated

We pray thee, Lord, for all who are in isolated places, or by infirmity are confined to home or hospital. Bless to them the word of the Gospel over the air, and grant to them a full and consoling sense of they presence, that together with us they may be strengthened and uplifted by thy gift of grace.

For Orphans and the Homeless

Lord Jesus, who in the days of thy flesh hadst no place to lay thy head, look, we beseech thee, with compassion upon all homeless folk and all children left without parental care. And that we do not fail them in their loneliness and need, inflame the hearts of our people with a spirit of concern for their welfare. Bless all homes for orphans, and all organizations working for the relief of human distress; and this we ask for thy Name's sake.

For the Blind and Deaf and Dumb

Almighty God, in whose Holy Word there is promise of a day when the eyes of the blind shall be opened, the ears of the deaf shall be unstopped, and the tongue of the dumb shall sing; of thy mercy, we beseech thee, for all who now live in darkness or in silence. Fortify them to bear their affliction with unwavering faith; grant to them that inner sight and hearing-ear to which thy truth and beauty are ever revealed; and may they know thee as their constant friend and guide.

For Alcoholics and Others

Gracious God, the helper of all who put their trust in thee, we pray for those who are enslaved by intoxicants or by some evil habit, especially   . Give them, O Lord, the desire and the will to be free, and the grace to continue in the right way; and show us how to help them and to lead them to thee who art our hope and strength.

For Sufferers

Heavenly Father, whose Blessed Son our Lord took upon himself our infirmities and had compassion upon all sick and suffering folk; Hear our prayer for all who suffer in body or mind or spirit; and especially we pray for   . Grant to them relief from pain, strength in their weakness, light in their darkness and, if it shall please thee, restoration to health. Enable them now to trust thee though thy way is hidden from their sight; and let them know that peace which is the gift of thy Holy Spirit.

For a Sick Child

Heavenly Father, who didst send thy beloved Son into the world in the form of a little child, and to whom all children are dear; watch, we pray thee, with us over   . In thy mercy ease *his* suffering and restore *him* to health again. Bless those who minister to *his* needs, and give to us who wait the help of thy grace.

A Prayer for the Sick With the Laying on of Hands

Lord, let the promise of Saint James that the prayer of faith would save the sick, be fulfilled now, as in thy Name we lay our hands on this thy servant (anointing *him*) for healing. Grant to *him* firm trust in thee; the quietness of confidence; and a will to rest *his* will contentedly in thine; through Jesus Christ our Lord.

For Those Who Serve the Sick

Blessed Lord, who went about doing good and healing all manner of sickness and infirmity, bestow thy blessing, we beseech thee, upon our doctors and nurses and all who work in hospitals and homes for the relief of human suffering. Give them skill and tenderness, cheerfulness and patience, and let them find their reward in grateful hearts and in the knowledge that they are serving thee.

For the Seemingly Incurable

O Lord, who dost feel the pain of the world; look with mercy, we beseech thee, upon those who in their sickness and suffering are beyond the reach of human skill. To thee alone belongs the power of life, and these souls are thine. If in the mystery of thy providence it shall be their lot to bear their infirmity to the end, then, Lord, of thy love give them grace to endure bravely, and such an assurance of thy presence with them in it that they may, like their Saviour, be made perfect through suffering.

For the Dying

Father of mercies and God of all comfort, we commit to thy gracious care and keeping this dear soul whose earthly day is ending and who is coming from us to thee. Receive *him,* Lord, whose hope is in thee; all sins forgiven, and the fulness of joy and peace made sure for *him* in continuing service in thy heavenly kingdom; through Jesus Christ our Lord.

For the Departed

O God, whose mercies cannot be numbered, accept our prayers on behalf of the soul of thy servant departed, and grant *him* an entrance into the land of light and joy, in the fellowship of thy saints; through Jesus Christ our Lord.

Remember thy servant, O Lord, according to the favour which thou bearest unto thy people, and grant that, increasing in knowledge and love of thee, *he* may go from strength to strength, in the life of perfect service in thy heavenly kingdom: through Jesus Christ our Lord, who liveth and reigneth with thee and the Holy Ghost ever, one God, world without end.

Grant, O Lord, to _____ eternal rest, and let thy light perpetual shine upon *him.*

For Those Who Mourn

Almighty God, Father of mercies and giver of all comfort, deal graciously, we pray thee, with all those who mourn, that, casting every care on thee, they may know the consolation of thy love; through Jesus Christ our Lord.

Grant, O Lord, to all who are bereaved the spirit of faith and courage, that they may have strength to meet the days to come with steadfastness and patience; not sorrowing as those without hope, but in thankful remembrance of thy great goodness in past years, and in the sure expectation of a joyful reunion with those they love; and this we ask in the Name of Jesus Christ our Saviour.

For Social Agencies

Almighty God, whose compassions fail not, and who hast taught us to have compassion upon those in need, prosper, we pray thee, the work of our social agencies, and especially our Community Chest. Stir up the wills of all our people to support them in the relief of want and suffering, and let us not rest until we have provided for the needs of thy children, giving generously as thou hast given to us.

O Lord, we pray that thou wilt hasten the time when no man shall live in contentment while he knows that his neighbor has need. Inspire in us and in all men the consciousness that we are not our own but thine and our neighbors', for his sake, who prayed that we might all be one in him—Christ Jesus our Lord.

For Animals

O God, who hast made all the earth and every creature that dwells therein; help us, we pray thee, to treat with compassion the living creatures entrusted to our care, that they may not suffer from our neglect nor become the victims of any cruelty. Bless all who serve in their behalf, and help us to find in caring for them a deeper understanding of thy love for all creation; through Jesus Christ our Lord.

For the Church

O Eternal God, who by thy Son Jesus Christ didst establish the family of thy Church in all the world, breathe upon it anew the gifts of thy Holy Spirit, that, ever awake to thy command, it may go forth in lowly service, yet in conquering might, to win mankind to the love of thy Name; through our only Saviour Jesus Christ.

Quicken, O Lord, we beseech thee, all the members of thy Church, that they may be alive to the opportunities and responsibilities of these times. Save us from complacency and from fear of new ways; inspire our minds with the vision of a world won for thee, and stir our wills to pray and to work until thy will is done on earth as it is in heaven.

For Church Councils

Almighty God, by whose Holy Spirit the Apostles were guided in their councils, direct, we beseech thee, the deliberations of our leaders and those who share with them the responsibility of planning and providing for the ongoing work of our Church. Grant to them wise judgment and adventurous faith, that they may lead us ever forward to greater service and achievement in the furtherance of thy kingdom in the world, until thy will is done on earth as it is in heaven and all mankind is one united family in thee; through Jesus Christ our Lord.

For Ministers

O Lord Jesus Christ, the good Shepherd, who didst lay down thy life for the sheep and appoint others to feed thy flock; give to our pastors the grace they need day by day faithfully to carry out the demanding duties of their sacred calling. Fill them with love for the souls committed to their care; inspire them with wisdom for the guidance and instruction of those who seek their aid; and in all things help them, and us whom they serve, to glorify thee by the good example of Christian lives; through Jesus Christ our Lord.

For a Local Church

O God, who hast brought us into the fellowship of thy dear Son, lead us all in this church ever closer day by day to thee and to one another, that we may become of one heart and mind in love toward thee; and grant that our common life and work in sacrificial service may help to extend thy kingdom here where we are and in all the world; through Jesus Christ our Lord.

For Children

Let thy love, O Lord, be so set before our children by lives of love, and thy holiness by good examples of virtue, that they may be led to love and serve thee all their days; through Jesus Christ our Lord.

For Church Schools

O God, our Heavenly Father, who through thy Son our Lord Jesus Christ, hast made known thy tender care for children, grant thy blessing, we beseech thee, upon our church schools. To those who teach give intelligence and patience, and to those who are taught the desire to learn and the will to walk in the

way of thy commandments; through Jesus
Christ our Lord.

For Theological Schools

Almighty God, our heavenly Father, who
are the only Source of light and life; send
down upon our Theological Schools the rich
gifts of thy good Spirit, that in them thy
truth may be sincerely sought, effectually received, and obediently followed, and that in
growing measure they may become centers of
inspiration and power. Endue their teachers
with wisdom, zeal and patience; inspire their
scholars with the spirit of truth, honor, and
humility; and grant that from all members of
the Church which they serve they may receive
willing and generous support; for the sake
of Jesus Christ our Lord.

For Missions

O God, who hast made of one blood all
the nations of men for to dwell on the face
of the whole earth; we give thee most humble and hearty thanks for the revelation of
thyself in thy Son Jesus Christ; for the commission to thy Church to proclaim the Gospel to every creature; for those who have
gone to the ends of the earth to bring light
to them that dwell in darkness and in the
shadow of death, and for the innumerable
company who now praise thy name out of

every kindred and nation and tongue. To thee be ascribed the praise of their faith for ever and ever.

O God, our heavenly Father, who didst manifest thy love by sending thine only begotten Son into the world that all might live through him; pour thy Spirit upon thy Church that it may fulfill his command to preach the Gospel to every creature; send forth, we beseech thee, laborers into thy harvest; defend them in all dangers and temptations; and hasten the time when all shall be saved; through the same thy Son, Jesus Christ our Lord.

For Missionaries

O most merciful Saviour, who willest that all men should be saved; be present with those who are gone forth in thy Name to preach the Gospel in distant lands (*especially*). Be with them in all perils, in sickness and distress, in weariness and painfulness, in disappointment and persecution. Give them sure confidence in thee. Pour out upon them abundantly thy Holy Spirit; and prosper mightily the work of their hands; send unto them faithful and true fellow-laborers. Give them a rich increase here, and grant that hereafter they may dwell with thee in the heavenly places, world without end.

For Mission Hospitals

O Lord, the Healer of all our diseases, who knowest how the sick have need of a physician, let thy perpetual providence guide and direct the work of mission hospitals throughout the world. Strengthen all whom thou hast called to be sharers in thine own work of healing; that the pain and grief of the world may be lightened, and the bounds of thy kingdom enlarged; through Jesus Christ our Lord.

For Educational Missions

O God, who art the goal of all knowledge and the source of all truth, who dost lead mankind towards thyself along the paths of discovery and learning, direct with thy wise Spirit the work of education in every land. Especially we would pray for those who have the difficult task of adapting western knowledge to the mind of eastern peoples. Give them insight into the needs of those whom they teach, humility to learn from their traditions, and wisdom to combine the old and the new. Above all, give them that grace and beauty of life without which all knowledge is vain; through Jesus Christ our Lord.

For Those in Religious Communities

Blessed Lord, who didst call thy disciples to follow thee in the way of sacrifice, we remember before thee those who have forsaken the natural pleasures and ambitions of life to devote themselves entirely to prayer and the service of thy holy Church. In their poverty, chastity and obedience be thou their wealth, their strength and stay, that in all things they may please thee and show forth thy glory before all men.

For Church Unity

O God, our Heavenly Father, whose blessed Son came to bring mankind into one family in thee; we pray for the unity of the Church in all the world. Help us to seek to heal the divisions which keep us from one another and weaken our efforts to extend thy kingdom in the earth. Give us understanding of other people's points of view; save us from prejudice; and grant that as we see clearly our Saviour's will that his Church may be one, so we may labor in love to bring it to pass; through Jesus Christ our Lord.

For the World Council of Churches

We thank thee, O Lord, for the World Council of Churches and for the hope and foretaste of the unity of thy people which it

For Lay-Workers

O Lord Jesus Christ, to whose service we are dedicated in thy holy Church, fit us, we beseech thee, for work we are given to do. Enlighten our minds as we study thy Holy Word; inspire us as we teach and preach; and make us good examples to others in holiness of life, to thy honor and glory.

Choosing a New Minister

Almighty God, we pray for the guidance of thy Holy Spirit as we seek a new Minister for our church. Thou knowest our special needs and the task that lies to our hand. In our search direct us, and give us insight to perceive the leader thou wouldst choose for us. And we further pray, O Lord, that in this time of waiting we may all devote ourselves afresh to thy service, so that nothing be lost of the faithful work of the past, but rather that it may be brought to a rich harvest in the years to come. This we ask in the Name of Jesus Christ our Lord.

For Church Officers

Blessed Lord, who hast called us to this office in thy Church, guide us, we beseech thee, in our deliberations, so that all our aims and purposes may be to the strengthening of the work in this church and the support of the Church's mission throughout the world; through Jesus Christ our Lord.

Institution of Officers in a Church Organization

O God, who by thy Holy Spirit didst endow the early disciples with varying gifts for the upbuilding and extension of the Church, each having a part to play according to their ability; we commend to thee now these thy servants who have been chosen for the responsible office of   in the of this church. Accept, O Lord, the willing offering of their time and talents; may thy Holy Spirit enable them to discharge their duties faithfully and well, and make their service fruitful to thy honor and glory; through Jesus Christ our Lord.

Dedication of Church School Teachers and Officers

Father of Mercy, whose Blessed Son, our Lord, laid upon his disciples a sense of responsibility for the care and well-being of children, we pray for thy blessing upon these thy servants who have offered themselves for the service of Christian nurture in our Church School. We thank thee for the privilege that is theirs and ours in sharing in this early training of our children in Christian faith and life. Endue them with insight and the Church's mission throughout the world; through Jesus Christ our Lord.

Institution of Officers in a Church Organization

O God, who by thy Holy Spirit didst endow the early disciples with varying gifts for the upbuilding and extension of the Church, each having a part to play according to their ability; we commend to thee now these thy servants who have been chosen for the responsible office of   in the   of this church. Accept, O Lord, the willing offering of their time and talents; may thy Holy Spirit enable them to discharge their duties faithfully and well, and make their service fruitful to thy honor and glory; through Jesus Christ our Lord.

Dedication of Church School Teachers and Officers

Father of Mercy, whose Blessed Son, our Lord, laid upon his disciples a sense of responsibility for the care and well-being of children, we pray for thy blessing upon these thy servants who have offered themselves for the service of Christian nurture in our Church School. We thank thee for the privilege that is theirs and ours in sharing in this early training of our children in Christian faith and life. Endue them with insight and

For Mission Hospitals

O Lord, the Healer of all our diseases, who knowest how the sick have need of a physician, let thy perpetual providence guide and direct the work of mission hospitals throughout the world. Strengthen all whom thou hast called to be sharers in thine own work of healing; that the pain and grief of the world may be lightened, and the bounds of thy kingdom enlarged; through Jesus Christ our Lord.

For Educational Missions

O God, who art the goal of all knowledge and the source of all truth, who dost lead mankind towards thyself along the paths of discovery and learning, direct with thy wise Spirit the work of education in every land. Especially we would pray for those who have the difficult task of adapting western knowledge to the mind of eastern peoples. Give them insight into the needs of those whom they teach, humility to learn from their traditions, and wisdom to combine the old and the new. Above all, give them that grace and beauty of life without which all knowledge is vain; through Jesus Christ our Lord.

For Those in Religious Communities

Blessed Lord, who didst call thy disciples to follow thee in the way of sacrifice, we remember before thee those who have forsaken the natural pleasures and ambitions of life to devote themselves entirely to prayer and the service of thy holy Church. In their poverty, chastity and obedience be thou their wealth, their strength and stay, that in all things they may please thee and show forth thy glory before all men.

For Church Unity

O God, our Heavenly Father, whose blessed Son came to bring mankind into one family in thee; we pray for the unity of the Church in all the world. Help us to seek to heal the divisions which keep us from one another and weaken our efforts to extend thy kingdom in the earth. Give us understanding of other people's points of view; save us from prejudice; and grant that as we see clearly our Saviour's will that his Church may be one, so we may labor in love to bring it to pass; through Jesus Christ our Lord.

For the World Council of Churches

We thank thee, O Lord, for the World Council of Churches and for the hope and foretaste of the unity of thy people which it

affords. Grant thy blessing upon all its effor toward united Christian thought and actio guide its leaders in council, and to all members give the spirit of fellowship a the will to find a way to the healing of our divisions, that so, at last, we may all truly one in thee, and glorify thee in all t world.

For the Nation

Almighty God, we beseech thee to lo with favor upon our land and people. undeserving, thou hast made us great amo the nations of the earth. Let us not for that this place and this power have come thee, and that we have them as a trust to in thy service. Save us from pride and a gance; make us quick to see the needs of th less fortunate than ourselves, and to be re lute in purpose to promote goodwill fellowship among all men; through Je Christ our Lord.

For Those in Authority

O Lord God Almighty, guide, we thee, our President and all those to wh has been committed the government of nation, and grant to them special gifts wisdom and understanding, of counsel strength; that upholding what is right, understanding, with patience and love; and when the going is hard, grant to them the secret job that comes of faithful continuance in the undertaken task, even as our Lord Jesus Christ, in whose Name we make our prayer.

For Church Organizations

O Lord, whose holy apostle has taught us that as members of thy body we all have our part to play in the whole life of thy Church, we thank thee for this work which thou hast given us to do together; and we pray thee to give us grace to persevere in it, and through it to serve thee to thy honor and glory.

For the Annual Canvass

O God, who hast been pleased to call us to be workers together with thee, make us now of one heart and mind to pray and work and give for the up-building and strengthening of thy Church at home and abroad. Bless our annual canvass, and stir up the wills of all our people to do according to their ability as good stewards in thy service; through Jesus Christ our Lord.

For an Annual Church Meeting

Grant, O Lord, that thy Holy Spirit may preside over us now in all our concerns and deliberations for the welfare of this church. We thank thee for all the blessings of the past year, and pray that we may go together from strength to strength in the year before us. Help us all to dedicate ourselves to thee, and to be ready to make sacrifice of time and money for the extension of thy kingdom.

Guide us, we beseech thee, in the choice of our officers, and may they discharge their duties faithfully.

We praise thee for those thy servants who labored and worshipped here before us, and especially for those who have departed this life since we last met together. Grant to them eternal rest, O Lord, and let thy light perpetual shine upon them; through Jesus Christ our Lord.

A Birthday Offering for Children

Lord Jesus, who didst show thy love for children by taking them into thy arms and giving them thy blessing; Bless also these children now here before thee with their gifts of thanksgiving for their birthday. We commend them to thy sustaining grace, and pray that thou wilt ever be their friend and companion through the years to come, and that they may follow thee faithfully to their life's end.

For a Church Building Campaign

Almighty God, who hast promised that wheresoever thy Name is recorded thou wilt come with thy blessing, look with favor, we beseech thee, upon our endeavors to build a sanctuary in this place worthy of thy holy Name. And do thou move the hearts and wills of all to give and serve until our purpose is accomplished, to thy honor and glory; through Jesus Christ our Lord.

Dedication of Church Furnishings

Lord God of our Fathers, who of old didst accept the willing offerings of thy people for the service and the beautifying of the sanctuary, we pray thee to accept and bless *this* (these   ) which we now dedicate for our use and to thy glory in our worship of thee. We thank thee for the faith and devotion of thy servant(s) by whom (or *for whom*) these gifts were made; and we commend them to thy constant care and keeping; through Jesus Christ our Lord.

For a Mission

Almighty God, who didst send thy Son into the world to save sinners and to lead us into the way of righteousness, bestow thy blessing, we beseech thee, upon our endeavour to bring souls to thee through this Mission and draw us ourselves to deeper consecration. May thy Holy Spirit inspire *him* who shall speak thy word, convince the indifferent, convert the wayward, and in all of us renew the will to do thy will and to continue steadfastly in thy service in the fellowship of thy holy Church, until thy will is done on earth as it is in heaven; through Jesus Christ our Lord.

For a Theological School

O Lord Jesus Christ, in whom is Truth and Life, let thy presence abide in our School; that seeking thy Truth we may find thee, and sharing thy Life, may dwell together in perfect fellowship, and in days to come be found faithful servants of thee, to whom, with the Father and the Holy Spirit, be glory and praise, now and forever.

For a Commencement

Prosper, we beseech thee, O Lord, the work of all our schools and colleges. Grant that all who teach and learn therein may set thy

holy will ever before them, and seek that
wisdom and understanding which are better
than the riches of the world. And herein
especially we pray for thy blessing upon this
school and upon those who now pass from its
walls into new spheres of learning and work.
May thy Fatherly hand ever be over them and
thy Holy Spirit ever be with them, and lead
them in the way of truth and of honorable
service, until they come to thy everlasting
kingdom; through Jesus Christ our Lord.

For a Business or Service Club

Almighty God, whose great commandment
is that we shall love our neighbors as ourselves, and who hast taught us that we should
do to others as we would have them do to us,
we ask thy blessing upon the work of this
Club. As our purpose is to help our fellow-
men and to promote all that is good in the
life of our community, so we pray that thou
wilt strengthen our hands in all our under-
takings, and that our work may spread the
spirit of fellowship and goodwill among all
men.

Grace for a Patriotic Banquet

We thank thee, Lord, for these thy earthly
gifts, and for all the blessings of this life.
Especially now, we give thee thanks for our
country: for those who laid its foundations,

and for those who have sacrificed their lives in its service. Strengthen, we pray thee, those who now labor to keep it strong; and do thou thyself be our defence against all our enemies, so that peace and harmony may ever flourish among us, and spread from us throughout the world.

For Thanksgiving Day

Almighty God, we thank thee for all the blessings of this life, and today especially for those that are ours in this free land; for the fruits of the soil, the untold resources of the earth, the opportunities for work and play and healthful living; for liberty in speech and written word; for public education and regard for every man's welfare. And we pray thee that, as we thank thee for these and all thy mercies, thou wilt continue thy good hand upon us and make our nation great in that greatness which alone is pleasing to thee, even the righteousness that is the doing of thy holy will.

For a National Observance

We thank thee, O Lord, for thy continued blessings to our peoples in this western world. We thank thee for the pioneers who opened the way, and for those who laid the foundations of our national life. Grant that we may ever dedicate ourselves to the unfinished work they so nobly advanced, and give increased devotion to the cause for which they gave the last full measure of devotion: that government of the people, by the people, for the people, shall not perish from the earth. With malice toward none, with charity for all, with firmness in the right as God gives us to see the right, let us strive on to finish the work we are in; to bind up the nation's wounds, to care for all who need our care, and to do all which may achieve and cherish a just and lasting peace among ourselves and with all nations.

Before an Election

Almighty God, who dost hold us to account for the use of all our powers and privileges; guide us, we pray thee, in the election of our leaders and representatives; that by wise legislation and faithful administration the rights of all may be protected, and our nation enabled to fulfil thy purposes; through Jesus Christ our Lord.

In a Time of Civil Strife

Lord, give us the grace to put ourselves in other people's places: to see ourselves as others see us. Save us from family strife that comes from self-will or lack of understanding, and help us to seek together a way to work together for the rights and liberties of all in responsible community life and service. As thou art the Father of us all, so let us live as members of one family in mutual consideration and concern for love of thee.

IN TIME OF WAR

For a Will to Peace

Almighty God, by whose grace we look for the day when nation shall not any more lift up sword against nation, and when men shall live without fear in security and peace, grant to us in this time of strife the will to labor for peace even while our sword is drawn to resist the oppressor. Let not the evil we oppose turn us from our purpose to achieve unity and concord among the nations of the earth, to thy honor and glory; through Jesus Christ our Lord.

For Chaplains in the Armed Forces

Blessed Lord, who didst commission thy disciples to continue the work which the Father sent thee into the world to do, support, we beseech thee, with thy Holy Spirit, those who minister in the Armed Forces of our country. Give them grace to preach thy Gospel both by word and deed; strengthen them in their temptations and make them courageous in the perils of their calling, that they may glorify thee before all men; and do thou hold them ever in thy gracious keeping.

For the Medical Services

O Lord, merciful Physician of souls, let thy blessing rest, we beseech thee, upon our medical services in the theater of war. Give to the doctors, nurses, stretcher-bearers, orderlies and Red Cross workers a full measure of thy enabling grace, that they may not grow weary in well-doing, but continue steadfastly in their work of mercy; and grant that through their labors many may be saved.

For the Wounded and the Fallen

Heavenly Father, we commit to thy gracious keeping the sick and wounded, the missing and prisoners of war. Be thou their strength and consolation; and in thy love and mercy, we beseech thee, receive the fallen to thyself, forgiving them their sins for thy Name's sake; through Jesus Christ our Lord.

For the Bereaved

Almighty God, who didst offer thy only Son to be made perfect through suffering, and to win our salvation by enduring the cross; sustain with thy healing power all those whose loved ones have given their lives in the service of our country. Redeem, we pray thee, the pain of their bereavement, that knowing their loss to be the price of our freedom, they may remember the gratitude of the nation for which they gave so costly a sacrifice. And grant, O Lord, that these dead shall not have died in vain, and that out of the distress of this present age there may arise a new and better world in which thy will shall rule, to the honor of thy Son, our Saviour Jesus Christ.

FOR HOLY COMMUNION

Psalm 15

Lord, who shall dwell in thy tabernacle? or who shall rest upon thy holy hill?

Even he that leadeth an uncorrupt life, and doeth the thing which is right, and speaketh the truth from his heart.

He that hath used no deceit in his tongue, nor done evil to his neighbour, and hath not slandered his neighbour.

He that setteth not by himself but is lowly in his own eyes, and maketh much of them that fear the Lord.

He that sweareth unto his neighbour, and disappointeth him not, though it were to his own hindrance.

He that hath not given his money upon usury, nor taken reward against the innocent.

Whoso doeth these things shall never fall.

I will go unto the altar of God, even unto the God of my joy and gladness. I will offer the sacrifice of thanksgiving.

I Corinthians 11:23-29

The Lord Jesus, the same night in which he was betrayed, took bread:

And when he had given thanks, he brake it,

and said, Take, eat; this is my body, which is broken for you: this do in remembrance of me.

After the same manner also he took the cup, when he had supped, saying, This cup is the new testament in my blood: this do ye, as oft as ye drink it, in remembrance of me.

For as often as ye eat this bread, and drink this cup, ye do show the Lord's death till he come.

Wherefore whosoever shall eat this bread, and drink this cup of the Lord, unworthily, shall be guilty of the body and blood of the Lord.

But let a man examine himself, and so let him eat of that bread, and drink of that cup.

For he that eateth and drinketh unworthily, eateth and drinketh damnation to himself, not discerning the Lord's body.

Almighty and everlasting God, behold we approach the sacrament of thy only begotten Son, our Lord Jesus Christ. As sick, we come to the physician of life; as unclean, to the fountain of mercy; as blind, to the light of eternal splendour; as needy, to the Lord of heaven and earth.

We pray thee of the abundance of thine infinite mercy that thou wouldst vouchsafe to heal our sickness, to wash our foulness, to lighten our darkness, and to enrich our poverty, that we may receive the Bread of Angels, the King of Kings, the Lord of Lords, with such reverence and fear, such contrition and love, such faith and purity, such devotion and humility as is expedient for the welfare of our souls. And grant us, O most merciful God, so to receive the Body and Blood of thy dear Son Jesus Christ that we may be incorporated into his mystical body and ever reckoned among his members. And, O most loving Father, grant that him whom we now purpose to receive under a veil we may at length behold with open face, even thy beloved Son, who with thee and the Holy Ghost liveth and reigneth ever, one God, world without end.

Before the Cross of Christ we can only bow in penitence for our great sin, in adoration of the glory which we there behold, full of grace and truth; praying that, as we are judged by the Cross, so we may also be pardoned; and that the love of God may so flood our hearts, and fill our world, that all men may be drawn to Christ, their shattered fellowships remade, and a deeper and more lasting community established.

O Saviour of the world, who by thy cross and precious blood hast redeemed us:
Save us, and help us, we humbly beseech thee, O Lord.

72

On Entering Church

Heavenly Father, bless me and all who worship here or elsewhere today in the fellowship of thy holy Church. Help me to worship thee in spirit and in sincerity, and to receive thy holy Word in singleness of heart and mind; through Jesus Christ our Lord.

Merciful Father, I humbly approach thine altar, desiring to offer thee the sacrifice of praise and thanksgiving:

For thine honor and glory;

In remembrance of the death and passion of thy Son;

In intercession for thy whole Church; with thanksgiving for the grace and virtue of all thy Saints.

For the pardon of my sins and power to lead a new life;

And for *(here name any special request or intention)*.

Accept me, O God, and bless me for thy Name's sake.

At the Offertory

Come to me, O Lord, in this holy sacrament; feed me with the Bread of Life, and give me grace to unite myself with thee in thy self-offering for the salvation of mankind; through Jesus Christ our Lord.

Before Going to the Altar

Lord Jesus, eternal Word of God incarnate, who hast ascended into heaven, yet in the fulness of thy presence art with us now, humbly I adore thee.

After Holy Communion

Heavenly Father, I pray that this Holy Communion may be to me new life and salvation: an armour of faith and a shield of good resolution: the riddance of evil and the increase of virtue. Be thou my hope and confidence, my riches and my joy, my refuge and my help, in whom my heart and mind may remain fixed forever.

O Lord, who in this wonderful sacrament hast left us a memorial of thy Cross and Passion, grant us so to venerate the sacred mysteries of thy Body and Blood, that we may ever perceive within ourselves the fruits of thy redemption; who livest and reignest with the Father and the Holy Spirit, one God for ever and ever.

On Leaving Church

Grant, O Lord, that the lessons I have learned may take root in my heart; that I may remain faithful to the confession of my faith; and that, aided by thy continuing grace, I may put my faith to practice in my daily life; through Jesus Christ our Lord.

LITANIES AND MEDITATIONS

Litany of the Christian Life

These are the words of the holy Apostles: Let this mind be in you, which was also in Christ Jesus; who took upon him the form of a servant . . . and humbled himself, and became obedient unto death, even the death of the cross.

Lord, have mercy upon us, and give us the mind of Christ.

Bear ye one another's burdens, and so fulfil the law of Christ.

Lord, have mercy upon us, and give us the mind of Christ.

Whoso hath this world's goods, and seeth his brother have need, and shutteth up his heart of compassion from him, how dwelleth the love of God in him? . . . Let us not love in word, neither in tongue, but in deed and in truth.

Lord, have mercy upon us, and give us the mind of Christ.

Pure religion and undefiled before God and the Father is this: to visit the fatherless and widows in their affliction, and to keep himself unspotted from the world.

Lord, have mercy upon us, and give us the mind of Christ.

Add to your faith virtue; and to virtue knowledge; and to knowledge self-control; and to self-control patience; and to patience godliness; and to godliness brotherly kindness; and to brotherly kindness charity.

Lord, have mercy upon us, and give us the mind of Christ.

Let your citizenship be as it becometh the gospel of Christ.

Lord, have mercy upon us, and give us the mind of Christ.

Beloved, building up yourselves on your most holy faith, praying in the Holy Ghost, keep yourselves in the love of God, looking for the mercy of our Lord Jesus Christ unto eternal life.

A Litany of Remembrance

Heavenly Father, we wait upon thee now in trust and love, and in filial devotion to thy holy will. By all thy works; by the remembrance of all thy mercies; by the revelation of thyself to the prophets of old:

Teach us, and draw us ever nearer to thee.

By the memory of Jesus Christ our Lord; by his life and teaching; by his life laid down for our salvation, and by the work of his Spirit in the world:

Teach us, and draw us ever nearer to thee.

By the noble example of all the saints and martyrs of the Church; by all that we owe to Christian faith and devotion down the years:

Teach us, and draw us ever nearer to thee.

By the joys of life; by human love; by the affection and fidelity of friends; by the capacity for pleasure, and the sense of humor; by the persistence in our hearts of optimism and hope:

Teach us, and draw us ever nearer to thee.

By the sorrows of life; by our falls and failures; by our disappointments and disasters; by the stern discipline of loneliness, of unrealized dreams, and the heartache of unsatisfied desire:

Teach us, and draw us ever nearer to thee.

By our want of thee; by the hunger within us for the eternal life; by our search for truth, and by our hands outstretched in prayer:

Teach us, and draw us ever nearer to thee.

The Lord's Prayer

Litany of the Will of God

Jesus said: *Not every one that saith unto me, Lord, Lord, shall enter into the kingdom of heaven, but he that doeth the will of my Father who is in heaven.*

Whosoever shall do the will of God, the same is my brother, and my sister, and mother.

O God, who hast made us for thyself and called us to work with thee in thy eternal purpose:

Thy will be done on earth as it is in heaven.

O God, whose will it is that thy Name and salvation shall be known in all the world:

Thy will be done on earth as it is in heaven.

O God, whose will it is that all men should know the truth that sets them free:

Thy will be done on earth as it is in heaven.

O God, whose purpose is to draw all men together as one family in Christ:

Thy will be done on earth as it is in heaven.

O God, who hast charged us to seek thy kingdom first, and to love thee with all our hearts and minds and our neighbors as ourselves:

Thy will be done on earth as it is in heaven.

From all unwillingness to learn thy will; from clinging to our own plans and desires; from all want of faith in thy purpose:

Save us, O God.

From refusal to follow thy will for us when we see it; from blinding ourselves to thy call by our own ambitions; from the shame of

79

turning back when once we have set out in the way of discipleship:

Save us, O God.

O Lord Jesus Christ, who by thy delight in doing thy Father's will, and by thy faithfulness to it even unto death, hast left us an example that we should follow in thy steps, give us grace to follow courageously and faithfully where thou hast led the way, for thy Name's sake.

A Litany for Christian Unity

(The following is based on a prayer written by Abbe Paul Couturier of France for use by Roman Catholics in a Week of Prayer for Christian Unity. We have changed the terms where necessary; the temper remains noteworthy.)

For our controversies often full of ironies, of narrowness of spirit or of exaggeration with regard to our non-Christian brethren, for our intransigences and for our severe judgments . . . *we beg thy pardon, Lord.*

For all the culpable violence which may have been exercised in history among Christian brethren . . . *we beg thy pardon, Lord.*

For all the proud or complacent attitudes which we have manifested through the centuries towards our Christian brothers, and for all our lack of comprehension in this respect . . . *we beg thy pardon, Lord.*

Above linguistic, racial, national . . . frontiers, unite us, Jesus . . . Above our ignorance, our prejudices, our instinctive enmities . . . *unite us, Jesus.*

O God, so that there may be one fold and one Shepherd . . . *gather the dispersed Christians.*

O God, in order that peace may at last reign in the world . . . *gather the dispersed Christians.*

O God, for the greatest joy in the heart of thy Son . . . *gather the dispersed Christians.*

For the Lenten Season

Blessed Lord, help me to go into the wilderness of quiet and meditation with thee during these forty days. Give me grace to examine myself honestly, and to put away everything that has been keeping me from following thee faithfully.

Almighty God, who hast said that man shall not live by bread alone but by thee, enable me to still all earthly desires, and to long only for those things which truly satisfy the soul.

O Holy Spirit, by whose aid alone we can be masters of ourselves, abide in me and give me self-control. Strengthen me to keep my tongue from angry and unkind words, and my body always as a temple meet for thee.

Heavenly Father, whose Blessed Son taught us to be perfect in love as thou art, help me to love my neighbors as myself. May the compassionate heart of Jesus ever be my inspiration and example, that thy love may be glorified by mine.

Lord Jesus, who didst demand of thy disciples that they should take up the Cross and follow thee, let me not falter in my self-denial before this stern discipline. Whatever sacrifice thou wouldst have me make for thee, give me grace to make it with a willing and joyful heart.

Holy Week

Blessed Saviour, as I follow thee through these holy days of thy Passion: the betrayal, the agony in the Garden, the trials and mocking and scourging, and the dread hours upon the Cross, quicken in me the spirit of sincere repentance for all my sins and a will to love and serve thee all the days of my life.

Meditation for Holy Week

Almighty God, our Heavenly Father, grant to us now, we beseech thee, as we follow our Blessed Lord through the days of his passion, a mind and a will to follow him faithfully all our days.

Jesus said: *The Son of Man came not to be ministered unto, but to minister and to give his life a ransom for many.*

And Jesus entered into Jerusalem, and into the temple: and when he had looked round about upon all things, and now the eventide was come, he went out unto Bethany with the twelve.

And they come to Jerusalem: and Jesus went into the temple, and began to cast out them that sold and bought in the temple, and overthrew the tables of the money changers, and the seats of them that sold doves . . . And he taught, saying unto them, Is it not written, My house shall be called of all nations the house of prayer? but ye have made it a den of thieves.

And as they did eat, Jesus took bread, and blessed, and brake it, and gave to them, and said, Take, eat; this is my body. And he took the cup, and when he had given thanks, he gave it to them: and they all drank of it. And he said unto them, This is my blood of the new testament, which is shed for many.

Jesus knowing that the Father had given all things into his hands, and that he was come from God, and went to God; he riseth from supper, and laid aside his garments; and took a towel, and girded himself. After that he poureth water into a basin, and began to wash the disciples' feet, and to wipe them with the towel wherewith he was girded.

And they came to a place which was named Gethsemane: and he saith to his disciples, Sit ye here, while I shall pray. And he taketh with him Peter and James and John, and began to be sore amazed, and to be very heavy: and saith unto them, my soul is exceeding sorrowful unto death: tarry ye here, and watch. And he went forward a little, and fell on the ground, and prayed that, if it were possible, the hour might pass from him. And he said, Abba, Father, all things are possible unto thee; take away this cup from me: nevertheless, not what I will, but what thou wilt.

And when they were come to the place, which is called Calvary, there they crucified him, and the malefactors, one on the right hand, and the other on the left. Then said

Jesus, Father, forgive them; for they know not what they do.

And when the sixth hour was come, there was darkness over the whole land until the ninth hour. And at the ninth hour Jesus cried with a loud voice, saying, Eloi, Eloi, lama sabachthani? which is, being interpreted, My God, my God, why hast thou forsaken me? And when Jesus had cried with a loud voice, he said, Father, into thy hands I commend my spirit: and having said thus, he gave up the ghost.

Lord, have mercy upon us.
Christ, have mercy upon us.
Lord, have mercy upon us.

Blessed Saviour:
By thy entry into Jerusalem:
Give us courage to accept the issues of our faith.

By thy cleansing of the Temple:
Give us zeal for righteousness and for thy holy Church.

By thy Breaking of the Bread and Giving of the Cup:
Help us to give ourselves for the life of the world.

By thy washing of the disciples' feet:
Take away our pride, and endue us with the spirit of true humility.

By thy acceptance in the Garden of the Will of God:
Help us to seek to learn the will of God, and to surrender our own will to it.

By thy forgiveness of those who nailed thee to the Cross:
Make us ready to forgive.

By thy faithfulness unto death, even the death of the Cross:
Make us steadfast in our faith to our life's end, for thy Name's sake.

Almighty and everlasting God, who, of thy tender love towards mankind, hast sent thy Son, our Saviour Jesus Christ, to take upon him our flesh, and to suffer death upon the cross, that all mankind should follow the example of his great humility; Mercifully grant, that we may both follow the example of his patience, and also be made partakers of his resurrection; through the same Jesus Christ our Lord.

BENEDICTIONS

Unto God's gracious mercy and protection we commit ourselves. The Lord bless us and keep us. The Lord make his face to shine upon us and be gracious unto us. The Lord lift up the light of his countenance upon us, and give us peace, both now and for evermore.

Now unto him who is able to do exceeding abundantly above all that we ask or think according to the power that worketh in us, unto him be glory in the Church and in Christ Jesus throughout all ages, world without end.

Go forth into the world in peace; be of good courage; hold fast that which is good; render to no man evil for evil; strengthen the fainthearted; support the weak; help the afflicted; honor all men. Love and serve the Lord rejoicing in the power of the Holy Spirit. And the blessing of God Almighty, the Father, the Son, and the Holy Ghost be upon you and remain with you for ever.

The God of all grace, who hath called us unto his eternal glory by Christ Jesus, make you perfect, stablish, strengthen, settle you. And to him be glory and dominion for ever and ever.

Peace be with you all that are in Christ Jesus.

INDEX